LET THE FIELDS REJOICE
Biblical Meditations
On Nature

Will Soll

DISCIPLESHIP RESOURCES

MATERIALS FOR GROWTH IN CHRISTIAN FAITH AND LIFE

P.O. Box 189 • Nashville, TN 37202 • Phone (615) 340-7284

ISBN 0-88177-104-X

Library of Congress Card Catalog No. 91-71796

DR104B

To the members of
First Presbyterian Church, Branson, Missouri,
and to the memory of
Janice Ann Miller, 1953-1991

Contents

Foreword

We live in the midst of ecological dangers and disasters serious enough to warrant the term *crisis*. Actually, it's worse than a crisis in two ways. First, a crisis usually implies something of relatively short duration, and nobody thinks this environmental "crisis" is going to go away any time soon. Second (perhaps related to the first), we are not responding as if to a crisis. In the face of repeated warnings from scientists and moralists, we have carried on business as usual.

This book does not purport to offer a solution to our ecological crisis. In the first place, it is a book to be used by small groups in churches to carry on discussion. As such, it needs to leave space for the readers' thoughts, concerns, and initiatives. In the second place, its subject matter is the Bible's view of nature, and the Bible is simply not a sufficient resource to deal with all the questions posed by the ecological crisis.

But while the Bible is not sufficient, it is necessary. It is necessary for Christians to ponder the Bible's perspectives on nature if they are going to have motivation and vision to respond to a "crisis" that will assuredly last a lifetime. I say this despite my own questions and reservations about what the Bible has to say on the subject. I expect that others among my readers will have questions and reservations too, though not necessarily the same as my own. But I also think that many are unaware of just how much direction the Bible can give us on this matter. If this little book makes members of Christ's church aware of how the resources in scripture can enlighten, surprise, challenge, and restrain us as we confront our long-term ecological crisis, then it will have served its purpose.

The book is designed to be used as a resource for six sessions, each about an hour long (although it can, of course, be adapted to other uses). Each session consists of meditations on some biblical passages and themes, interspersed with questions. The meditations can be read before or during the session, but they should be read by all participants (not just the leader). There is space in this resource for individuals to write their answers to the questions.

Biblical quotations are taken from the New Revised Standard Version, except where noted. In a few instances I have used my own translation of the text (indicated by the abbreviation "auth. trans."). Explanatory notes are indicated by one or two asterisks and are found at the bottom of the page; sources for quotations are given in endnotes at the back of the book.

This book would not have been possible without the patient encouragement and editorial oversight of Dr. Craig Gallaway of Discipleship Resources, and was almost as much fun as our mandolin-guitar collaborations in graduate-school days. It is dedicated to the members of Branson First Presbyterian Church. Members of the adult class there will recognize those portions of the book which had their "debut" there; the portions that are less familiar in a sense owe even more to our time together. In particular, I would like to thank Debra Jones and Dr. Stephen Miller, who helped me teach the class and who offered useful suggestions on the manuscript. Dr. William Trollinger, always a helpful friend, also read the book and made valuable comments. I am grateful to Joe Sheldon for his bibliographic assistance.

As I leave this church family for St. Louis, I take my immediate family—wife Shari and daughters Amy and Katy—with me. They are so much a part of everything I do that expressing my thanks to them for their forbearance, wisdom, and love seems superfluous. Yet we miss a great deal of life if we fail to acknowledge and value the obvious. That, in a sense, is what this book is all about.

Will Soll
Branson, Missouri

Shevuos, 5751
"The festival of harvest, . . .
of what you sow in the field" (Ex. 23:16).

Pentecost, 1991
"You send forth your Spirit . . .
and you renew the face of the ground"
(Ps. 104:30).

Study #1

THE HOPE OF THE GOSPEL AND HOPE FOR THE WORLD

THE KINGDOM IN OUR MIDST

"This world is not my home, I'm just a-passing through."[1] So begins an American hymn. And many Americans, Christians included, have treated the world with a disregard typical of the most thoughtless tourists, who go to a place and leave it the worse for their visit.

The world in this hymn is seen as a stopping place on the way to our "true home." In a sense, this attitude toward the world is appropriately Christian. But is it all Christianity has to offer?

The study of the Gospels would suggest otherwise. The primary focus of Jesus' teaching is not how to get out of this world as neatly and cleanly as possible, but the proclamation of "the good news of the kingdom of God" (Luke 8:1). Matthew's Gospel prefers the term *kingdom of heaven*, which is synonymous with "kingdom of God." Heaven was a characteristically Jewish way of referring to God, as when the prodigal son confesses to his father, "I have sinned against heaven" (Luke 15:21).

The term *kingdom of God/kingdom of heaven* is richly suggestive, and it would distract us from our purpose to attempt to define it too precisely. But we can erect at least one hedge against misunderstanding. The kingdom of heaven does not refer to going to heaven when you die. True, Jesus told the criminal on the cross, "Today you will be with me in Paradise" (Luke 23:43). But when he talked about "the kingdom of heaven," he was talking about something else.

Jesus spoke of the kingdom of God not in terms of our going out of this world to God, but in terms of God coming to us and ruling in a new way in the world. Thus the kingdom could be said to be "at hand" (Matt. 4:17), as a budding movement whose inconspicuous beginnings would have universal results (Matt. 13:31-39), a movement capable of educating those who are loyal to it (Matt. 13:52). The same people who receive the kingdom shall "inherit the earth" (Matt. 5:3-5). Jesus' hearers are concerned with when the "kingdom of God" will appear (Luke 17:20; 19:11); Jesus encourages them to perceive its incipient growth as something that is already "among" them* (Luke 17:21; also Mark 4:26-29).

---

*This verse is often mistranslated as "the kingdom of God is within you."

1

Some Christians believe that divine rule will be established through God's direct intervention at the end of history. Others believe that the manifestation of God's kingdom occurs as a gradual process through the life of God's people. Some are frankly unsure if they can endorse any scenario for the coming of the kingdom of God.

Perhaps it will help us appropriate Jesus' teaching about the kingdom of God if we have a vision of the kingdom that is less a "scenario" and more a claim—a claim which we believe God will vindicate even if we are not sure how. The claim, simply put, is that "the earth is the Lord's" (Ps. 24:1; 1 Cor. 10:26); that God has "put all things under [Christ's] feet" (Eph. 1:22).

This is not a rose-colored view in which the world is seen as practically perfect. It is obvious that all things are not as God would have them. The claim of Christ's kingdom is staked against present abuses of power and authority. And that includes the abuse of the earth.

When Christians are commanded, "Do not love the world or the things in the world" (1 John 2:15), it may seem that this kind of committed love of nature is prohibited. But in the next verse, the writer tells us what he means when he talks about the "world"—the lust, greed, and arrogance that constitute the spirit of the present age. It is this atmosphere—so prevalent in the world and so ruinous to nature—that we are called to repent of that we might claim the world for Christ.

QUESTIONS

1. "Christians are too heavenly minded to be any earthly good" (anonymous). "Because we love something else more than this world we love even this world better than those who know no other" (C. S. Lewis).[2] In the light of the church's performance in confronting the environmental crisis, which statement rings more true? Can you think of any examples in the history of the church of each of these positions?

In the lives of Christians known to you personally?

2. How do you perceive God at work in the world today?

WORTHY IS THE LAMB

If the earth is included in Christ's kingdom, the redemption wrought by Christ affects the earth also. The New Testament affirms this in a number of ways. Romans 8 contains a discussion of Christian hope in the light of the liberation from sin achieved by Christ. In 8:18-25, Paul discusses the consequences of this liberation for nature itself, stating that nature "waits with eager longing for the revealing of the children of God" in order that it may be "set free" and share in their liberty.

But no vision of nature's participation in God's kingdom is more forceful than the initial vision of John in the Book of Revelation. The vision dramatizes not only nature's praise of God, but its joy at the reign of Christ.

John sees God seated on a throne from which issue flashes of lightning and peals of thunder (4:2, 5). This ancient imagery associates God with the power of the storm, which can be terrible, but more often beneficial for fertility. Around the throne are "twenty-four elders, dressed in white robes, with golden crowns on their heads" (4:4). We cannot say for certain who these twenty-four are; perhaps twelve represent Israel and twelve the church. In any case, the description of them as "elders" leads us to think in terms of some particular human community.

In contrast to the elders who represent a social realm, there are four "living creatures" who also give praise to God continually, and who represent the realm of nature: "The first living creature like a lion, the second living creature like an ox, the third living creature with a face like a human face, and the fourth living creature like a flying eagle" (v. 7). These of course are not ordinary representatives of their species, since they each have "six wings" and are "full of eyes." But, in the cosmic symbolism of John's vision, they represent the natural world just as the elders represent the social world: the lion representing wild animals, the ox representing domestic animals, humankind representing itself, and the eagle representing the birds. The imagery is derived from the first chapter of Ezekiel.* Through these "four living creatures," the world of nature offers its continual praise to God: "Holy, holy, holy the Lord God the Almighty, who was and is and is to come!" (4:8).

But all is not well, even in heaven. The course of the cosmos is apparently stalled, prevented from reaching its appointed end. The One on the throne holds a sealed scroll of destiny, and "no one in heaven or on earth or under the earth . . . was found worthy to open the scroll or to look into it" (5:3-4). The prophet is extremely sorrowful because of this, until he is told by one of the elders, "Do not weep. See, the Lion of the tribe of Judah, the Root of David, has conquered, so that he can open the scroll and its seven seals" (5:5). The prophet looks and sees not a lion, but "a Lamb standing as if it had been slaughtered" (5:6).

The one who is worthy to open the scroll is therefore both predator and prey, dead and yet alive. The richness of imagery for Christ in this passage prevents us from overly identifying him with any one point in the natural cycle. Because of his victory over evil, "every creature in heaven and on earth and under the earth and in the sea" cries out, "To the one seated on the throne and to the Lamb be blessing and

---

*No creeping things or sea creatures! Let us hope the omission was not intended as a slight. The roots of this sort of symbolism are complicated. Revelation, for example, employs an ancient mythic image of the sea as a source of chaos and evil, so that a "beast" from the sea (13:1) does not represent fish and whales, but the evil that is abroad on earth.

honor and glory and might forever and ever" (5:13). Lapwings and lizards, worms and whales, here acclaim not only their Maker, but their Savior.

To realize that the reign of Christ is joyfully hailed by "every creature in heaven and on earth and under the earth and in the sea" broadens our vision of the scope of Christ's kingdom. It reminds us that his redemption includes all of creation, and not merely humanity. That is why Isaac Watts, in his famous hymn "Joy to the World," wrote not only "let every heart prepare him room," but also, "and heaven and nature sing."

QUESTIONS

3. I recently saw a sweatshirt that accused human beings of acting as if they were the only species on the planet. What antidotes to this view are present in the New Testament passages discussed?

4. What is the value of using imagery of natural forces and creatures for God, as Revelation does?

5. J. B. Phillips paraphrases Roman 8:19 as, "The whole creation is on tiptoe to see the wonderful sight of the [children] of God coming into their own." Why would nature be so eager to see what's going to happen to us?

How is nature's redemption linked to humanity's redemption?

6. Is our current posture toward nature so abusive as to make our talk of "redeeming" nature meaningless, at least until we stop abusing it?

Study #2

THE OLD TESTAMENT, THE LAND, AND MORAL ECOLOGY

THE OLD FULFILLS THE NEW

In our last study, we saw that when Jesus spoke of the kingdom of God, he spoke of God's rule being manifest in this world; we also observed that the New Testament depicts Christ's redemption of all creation, not merely humanity. We have therefore strong reasons for believing that in protecting the environment from abuse, we are not only preserving our own life-support system, but doing the work of the kingdom of God.

It must be said, however, that the New Testament does not do very much to apply this insight to environmental problems. This is not merely because the environmental crisis as we know it is of modern manufacture. Belief in the reign of the risen Christ in heaven, while it could be used to claim the earth for Christ, could also be used to cultivate a taste for the heavenly *as opposed to* the earthly, the imperishable *as opposed to* the perishable.* For many early Christians, the time between the present evil age and the coming reign of Christ was not felt to be long. The main challenge was to persevere in fidelity to Christ. Challenges to that fidelity in their world came more from exalting the creature against the Creator (through the worship of idols) than from failing to appreciate the creation (through the worship of profits).

My task is not to blame or defend the New Testament here, but to explain why, having begun with the New Testament, we will now be turning to the Old. The Old Testament has more to say about this world as a home which we share with creatures than the New. Unlike the New Testament, which comes to us from congregations scattered throughout the Roman Empire, whose "citizenship is in heaven" (Phil. 3:20), the Old Testament comes to us from a people deeply attached to their land. Its wisdom concerning the realm of nature will help us flesh out the New Testament's inclusion of nature in the kingdom of God.

---

*Especially given the fear of "decay" in the Greco-Roman world. Contrast this fear with our own fear of products that *won't* decay!

This isn't the only area where the Old Testament enhances the New. For instance, in telling the story of the crucifixion of Jesus, the Gospel writers were heavily dependent on such Old Testament passages as Psalms 22 and 69, and Isaiah 53. In a sense, these passages were as much sources for their narrative as the reminiscences of Jesus' associates. Therefore, we should not deem it unworthy or second-rate if we go to the Old Testament to "flesh out" the bare bones of a New Testament assertion.

NO VISION WITHOUT PARTICULARS

We will, of course, be reading the Old Testament through New Testament eyes on certain points. The hope of a life beyond this one need not be a distraction to Christians with environmental concerns; in fact, it can motivate them to costly obedience when the situation appears bleakest. Moreover, Old Testament religion is by nature the religion of a particular nation; Christians, while they still have serious national concerns, have a primary loyalty to a church which transcends national boundaries. This means we will always be generalizing from a scripture that talks about a particular land and a particular people at a particular time.

But the "particularity" of the Old Testament is an opportunity rather than an obstacle. As a college professor of mine once observed, there is no vision without particulars.* We will therefore be learning to love "the earth" by contemplating Israel's love for that patch of land on which it lived.

Israel's love for its land is attested to many times in its scriptures. One characteristic passage comes from a speech that comes down to us as the speech of Moses just before Israel enters Canaan.

> The land which you are entering to occupy is not like the land of Egypt from which you have come, where, after you sowed your seed, you irrigated it by foot [probably with a waterwheel] like a vegetable garden. No, the land into which you are crossing to occupy is a land of hills and valleys that drinks in rain from the heavens, a land which the Lord your God looks after, whose eyes are upon it continually from the beginning of the year to the end. If, then, you truly heed my commandments which I enjoin on you today, loving and serving the

---

*He was lecturing about William Blake, a visionary British poet who was passionate on this point.

Lord your God with all your heart and soul, I will give rain for your land in season, the early rain [October or November] and the late rain [April and May], that you may have your grain, wine, and oil to gather in, and I will bring forth grass in the fields for your animals. Thus you may eat your fill (Deut. 11:10-15, auth. trans.).

In fact, the land to which the Lord led Israel has not been the envy of the ages—ancient geographers regard Egypt as having been more fertile than Canaan, not less. * But while this shows that the biblical writers were biased in favor of their home (as we all are), it also makes our passage generally applicable. For it is no paradise, but "ordinary" land that is praised in these terms. It is this land from which Israel is to get its grain (for food), its wine (for drink), and its multipurpose olive oil, † a familiar triad of blessings in the Old Testament (Deut. 7:13; Joel 2:24; Ps. 4:7). It is this land whose seasonal rains constitute the rhythm of Israel's life, rains which are understood as gifts from its covenant Lord.

QUESTION

1. Think of a place that you feel particularly attached to because of what exists there naturally. Why do you feel this attachment?

---

* In fact, as far as the Egyptians were concerned, the regular flooding of the Nile was the gods' preferred way of renewing the land; other nations had to have the inferior expedient of having "a Nile in the sky" (i.e., rain).

† Olive oil was used, among other things, as a basic component in bread making (1 Kings 17:12-16; Lev. 2) and as fuel for lamps (Exod. 27:20). In the Old Testament, most references to olive oil involve its application to the skin, to soften it and make it shine (Ps. 104:15). Sometimes such applications were specifically medicinal (Isa. 1:6), cosmetic (Esth. 2:12; Song 1:3), or ceremonial (1 Sam. 10:1), but they were by no means restricted to these. Oil was associated with gladness, to be avoided only when in mourning (2 Sam. 14:2); the author of Ecclesiastes advised his readers to always have oil on their heads (9:8).

What would you say to someone who described your attachment as merely sentimental?

Are the natural benefits of this place currently threatened? If so, how?

YOU SHALL BE SATISFIED

The benefits of the land are further described in another passage, in which the generous fruits of nature combine with human industry and enjoyment to create a picture of complete satiation (in the best sense of that word). The following references from Deuteronomy 8 come from *The Holy Scriptures: The New Jewish Publication Society Translation.*

The Lord your God is bringing you into a good land, a land with streams and springs and fountains issuing from plain and hill, a land of wheat and barley, of vines, figs, and pomegranates, a land of olive trees and honey; a land where you may eat bread without stint, where you will lack nothing; a land whose rocks are iron and from whose hills you can mine copper. When you have eaten your fill, give thanks to the Lord your God for the good land which He has given you (Deut. 8:7-10).

But Moses also realizes that such "satiation" carries with it the seeds of its own undoing:

> Take care lest you forget the Lord your God and fail to keep His commandments, His rules, and His laws, which I enjoin upon you today. When you have eaten your fill, and have built fine houses to live in, and your herds and flocks have multiplied, and your silver and gold have increased, and everything you own has prospered, beware lest your heart grow haughty and you forget the Lord your God—who freed you from the land of Egypt, the house of bondage; who led you through the great and terrible wilderness . . . in order to test you by hardships only to benefit you in the end—and you say to yourselves, "My own power and the might of my own hand have won this wealth for me." Remember that it is the Lord your God who gives you power to get wealth, in fulfillment of the covenant that He made on oath with your fathers (Deut. 8:11-18).

QUESTION

2. Moses expresses the dangers and temptations of satiation in terms of forgetting. What does he exhort Israel to remember?

What must we remember if we are to rightly value what we have?

IT SHALL GO WELL WITH YOU

In Deuteronomy, the continued enjoyment of the blessings of the land is based on loving and serving the Lord and heeding the commandments Moses enjoins on the people. Land, creatures, climate, and people are joined in an interlocking *moral ecology* overseen and undergirded by the Lord.

The word *ecology* does not occur in the Bible, but that which is studied in ecology—the interdependence of organisms with their living and nonliving environment—is explicitly described in a number of biblical passages. Moreover, a fundamental assumption of much of the Bible is that people have a special place in our ecosystem, and that the *moral* choices we make affect that ecosystem. We shall therefore use the term *moral ecology* to indicate that the moral choices we make affect the social and natural fabric of which we are a part.

Some would say that by imputing to humanity "moral choices" and a "special place," we have already committed ourselves to ravaging the environment: By making ourselves masters, we make ourselves abusers. I agree with parts of this argument, except that I would change "abusers" to "potential abusers." We will be more attuned to the biblical writings if we endeavor, not to deny humanity's special place, but to affirm the special responsibility that goes with it; not to dismiss the language of morality as pretentious, but to realize that decisions which affect the environment are moral choices.

The Bible describes this moral ecology in both general and specific terms. An example of the former is this indictment from the prophet Hosea, which links the devastation of nature to human crimes and failings:

> There is no fidelity, no tenderness,
> no knowledge of God in the country,
> only perjury and lies, slaughter, theft,
> adultery and violence, murder after murder.
> This is why the country is in mourning,
> and all who live in it pine away,
> even the wild animals and the birds of heavens;
> the fish of the sea themselves are perishing (4:2-3, JB).

As a specific application of this moral ecology, consider the following law from Deuteronomy:

If, while walking alone, you chance upon a bird's nest with young birds or eggs in it, in any tree or on the ground, and the mother bird is sitting on them, you shall not take away the mother bird along with her brood; you shall let her go, although you may take her brood away. It is thus [that you] shall have prosperity and a long life (Deuteronomy 22:6-7, NAB).

The concern here is not humanitarian (otherwise the law must apply to the young as well), but ecological. At stake in this law is the preservation of species of birds. Israel must not overtax or exhaust the rich but vulnerable web of life in which it finds itself.

What are we to make of the final phrase, "Thus it shall go well with you, and you shall live long"? A story is told of an ancient rabbi who lost his already-deteriorating faith when he saw someone drop dead shortly after he "let the mother bird go." But that rabbi had already lost touch with the fundamentally communal orientation of this text. In the Book of Deuteronomy, the "you" addressed in the phrase "it shall go well with you, and you shall live long" is Israel as a whole, and the promise refers to Israel's prolonged enjoyment of the land (Deut. 4:40; 6:2; and so on). The two other specific commandments which have this promise attached to them concern honoring parents (Exod. 20:12, Deut. 5:16) and using fair weights and measures in commerce (Deut. 25:13-15). It "goes well" with Israel when the nation observes these commandments because of the effect of such observance on the overall texture of community life, even if people as individuals are inconvenienced by their observance. The individual benefits, not as a self-contained recipient of divine favor, but as part of a community whose relations to its land and its Lord are harmonious.

The command thus encourages Israel to take a long view of its actions. This attitude was expressed recently by a homemaker/environmentalist who told an interviewer:

To try to find out the public good, I would try to ask questions about how this or that would affect the community twenty-five years from now. Not whether such and such a regulation will affect somebody else's pocketbook. The biggest problem we have in all areas of government is that people look to the immediate present rather than to the future.[3]

The moral ecology in which we participate links us not only to the rest of creation, but to subsequent generations.

QUESTIONS

3. Hosea 4:1-3 claims that the lack of "fidelity" and "tenderness" and the presence of lies, theft, and violence were responsible for the devastation of nature. How are these responsible for the devastation of nature in our time?

Is this the same kind of connection envisaged by Hosea?

4. If the promise "it shall go well with you" encourages us to take a long view of our ecological situation, what are the personal and public pressures that prevent us from taking this long view?

5. We have already examined a biblical law concerning the preservation of species. Another law protects fruit trees in time of war:

When you are at war with a city and have to lay siege to it for a long
time before you capture it, you shall not destroy its trees by putting
an ax to them. You may eat their fruit, but you must not cut down
the trees. After all, are the trees of the field people, that they should
be included in your siege? (Deut. 20:19, auth. trans.).

There is a humorous absurdity to the rhetorical question, "Are the
trees of the field people?" But what larger point or principle is being
made by this question?

6. The law goes on to permit the cutting of nonfruitbearing trees
for siegeworks (Deut. 20:20). Why do you think fruit trees* were
singled out for special protection?

7. Does nature have intrinsic rights? Or should we speak simply of
human rights to such things as clean air and water?

---

*NRSV translates "trees that produce food." Understanding this verse depends on how
broadly one understands the Hebrew *peri* which, like our English word *fruit,* can refer
either to a particular kind of food or, more broadly, to the result of a natural process.

8. We have twice gone to biblical laws for specific applications of ecological principles. Old Testament "law" is often deprecated in Christian circles in contrast to New Testament "grace." Are laws necessary for effective ecological action?

What are their limits?

Study #3

CREATION AND CHAOS

THE VULNERABLE WEB

In the last section, we saw how the Old Testament situated Israel in the midst of a rich but vulnerable web of life. Israel's choices could have an impact on this web for ill as well as for good, and we used the term *moral ecology* to describe this connection between Israel's choices and the well-being of the land and the other creatures on which Israel depended.

Yet this web can get torn for reasons over which we, individually and corporately, have no apparent control. Flood, fire, drought, pestilence—ancient Israel was threatened by a host of natural disasters whose impact was just as destructive as the impact of invasion and oppression. The vulnerability of the web of life, disturbing as it is to contemplate, cannot be glossed over.

These issues call into question the very terms we use in our discussion. For if the environmental movement is a movement to "save nature," just what is that "nature" we are trying to save? If our planet reverted to a lifeless condition, would that not be as "natural" as the condition of the numberless lifeless planets around us?

The term *nature* is far too common and has too many positive and useful connotations to be abandoned. But for the rest of this chapter, I will be using two different terms, both derived from biblical study: *creation* and *chaos*. Even here we will have to be careful, for these terms can suggest *static* visions of order and disorder, whereas the biblical language has, as we shall see, a much more *dynamic* background.

THE THREAT OF CHAOS

An ancient Babylonian creation story—at least as old as Genesis—depicts the world we know as the creation of a generation of younger gods who fought a group of older gods identified with the primeval waters. These waters wanted to overwhelm all else so that things would revert to the earlier state when the waters were all that was. From the slain carcass of Tiamat, the monstrous deity of the waters of chaos, Marduk, the champion of the "younger" gods, fashioned the world.

At first glance this all seems very removed from the biblical God, who has no genealogy, whose story of creation contains no monsters and no combat, and whose mastery of the world appears to be perpetually unchallenged. Nevertheless, it is noteworthy that when the curtain goes up on creation in Genesis 1, there is not a blank screen, but "darkness covered the face of the deep, while a wind from God swept over the face of the waters" (v. 2). It is over against this watery chaos that God goes about his creative activity.

Moreover, Genesis 1 is not the only text that talks about creation, and several biblical texts that do so allude to myths in which creation is linked to God's combat with a sea monster. In Psalm 74, God is said to have "smashed the heads of the dragons in the waters" and "crushed the heads of Leviathan" (74:13-14) as a necessary prelude to the creation of dry land, fresh water springs, day and night, and the seasons (74:15-17). The psalm concludes with a prayer which asks God to "rise up" to defeat the foe, citing the noise and uproar of the rebellious enemy forces. So even while the myth deals with primeval time, the identification of the enemy with the forces of chaos brings the myth to bear on the present crisis. "Chaos" is therefore not exclusively identified with natural forces. The malignant effects of flood and war are comparable: the sense of things coming apart, the rending of the web of life.

Even passages that lack a combat myth use imagery of "the waters" as a threat to the created order. In Psalm 93, God's reign is affirmed in opposition to their rebellious clamor:

> The waters have lifted up, O Lord,
>> The waters have lifted up their voice;
>> The waters have lifted up their tumult.
> Mightier than the roaring of the many waters,
>> Mightier than the breakers of the sea,
>> Mightier is the Lord who dwells on high (vv. 3-4, auth. trans.).

It may come as a surprise to us who know the importance of water in the development of life on our planet to see "the waters" so consistently portrayed as a threat. For the biblical writers, this flood imagery by no means blinded them to the many virtues of water. In its place, water was an integral part of a beneficent order. But they also saw its destructive potential when it became a flood.

Can this ancient mythic symbol still speak to us? That will be for you to decide as you proceed with this study. But notice that the drama implicit in this symbolism is far removed from a complacent, "God's in his heaven—all's right with the world!" attitude. The threats to life are real. Yet the faith of Israel is not in a God who justifies chaos, but in a God who overcomes chaos.

QUESTIONS

1. What aspects of life, beneficial in their place, have a destructive potential that you fear?

2. Do we sometimes perceive natural events as manifestations of "chaos," when in fact they ultimately promote life?

3. The imagery of chaos suggests that God's mastery of chaos and the creation of the web of life were not things Israel took for granted. Scholars suggest that these things were reaffirmed annually in a new year festival. How does the church affirm these things in its corporate worship, and what else can it do?

ORDER, DISTINCTION, AND INTERDEPENDENCE

While there is only the faintest echo of a divine combat with a primeval sea monster in Genesis 1, the allusions to this tradition here and elsewhere in the Bible provide us with a helpful background. In particular, it helps us realize that the central issue in that chapter is not existence vs. nonexistence, but chaos vs. life-promoting order.

Chaos in Genesis 1 is represented at the outset of the chapter by an expanse of "water, water everywhere": boundless, pointlessly swirling, with no distinction, form, or variation. God responds by introducing a series of separations: light from darkness (v. 4), waters above from waters below (v. 6), waters below from dry land (v. 9). This is not the "separation" of an apartheid state, designed to crush or exploit; it is rather the birth of identity. Vast as these realms are, they now have boundaries and limits, and harmonious interaction between them is now possible. These newly created realms are given names as a seal of their newborn identity: Day, Night, Sea, Sky, and Earth.

These realms become the basis for an increasingly differentiated creation which is described as the offspring of these realms: Note the phrases, "let the waters bring forth" (v. 20) and "let the earth bring forth" (v. 24; cf. vv. 11-12). These creatures fill the realms of earth, sea, and sky. Note the repeated emphasis on the variety of species as the narrator repeats the phrase "of every kind" six times in verses 21-25. *

---

*While neither the creation story nor any other biblical passage gives us a detailed list of species, we are given as a model of wisdom the example of Solomon who "would speak of trees, from the cedar that is in the Lebanon to the hyssop that grows in the wall; he would speak of animals, and birds, and reptiles, and fish" (1 Kings 4:33).

Many people wonder why Genesis 1 defers the creation of sun and moon until Day 4, *after* the vegetation has already appeared on earth. The answer is that Genesis 1 is much more concerned with the harmonious order of creation than it is with the chronology of its origins. The writer wants to show the connection of the realms that God creates in the first three-day sequence with the creatures that "fill" or "rule" them, which God creates in the second three-day sequence. The following chart should make the correspondences and connections clear.

REALMS	THEIR FILLERS/RULERS
Day 1	**Day 4**
Day	"great light" (sun)
Night	"lesser light" (moon)
	and the stars
Day 2	**Day 5**
Sky	birds
Sea *	sea creatures
Day 3	**Day 6**
Earth and its	land animals and humankind
vegetation	

Note that the sun and the moon are not even named, since in the world of Israel's neighbors their names were the names of deities. Thus, while they are given "rule" over the day and night, they are not to be confused with the God who created all, but are subordinate to God's purposes for all creation. Presumably, this same principle applies to the human beings made in God's image who are to "rule" over the earth, a topic which will receive detailed attention in our next chapter.

The delight in rhythm and pattern that we find in Genesis 1 bears witness to one who could see creation not only as marvelously ordered, but also as a kind of universal liturgy. However, these same features can mislead us if they cause us to understand this order statically rather than dynamically. Just as chaos was not merely disorder, but an active, destructive force, so the order which God brings into being is no mere set of slots, but a living, changing and interchanging network.

Again, it will help if we look at other texts that deal with creation; in this case, texts which emphasize God's creative involvement with the world as something which did not cease in primeval times, but is present and continual. Psalm 104 (which we will examine in detail in our final study) sees God's hand in the creation of every generation of

---

* Separated from sky on Day 2, though named on Day 3.

species, not just the primeval prototypes: "When you send forth your spirit, they are created; and you renew the face of the ground" (v. 30). At the end of the Book of Job, God presents Job with a catalog of divine involvement with nature, about which Richard Austin has written,

> Where we see predation and adaptation in an ecosystem of mutual support, the Hebrew poet saw the Lord directly feeding the lion and the raven, and acting as midwife for the successful birth of a fawn. This perspective need not embarrass modern Christians. We can appreciate how environmental systems are expressive of God's beauty in that the Lord *not only creates but bestows creativity upon the earth.*[4]

In Genesis 1, what God creates is itself creative. When God says, "Let the earth put forth vegetation," we do not sense that the earth's creativity is in competition with God's. Rather, earth's creativity is grounded in God's and is an extension of God's. Moreover, God addresses the command "Be fruitful and multiply" directly to the creatures; as with the humanity that is about to be created, God "speaks," and the creatures respond.

According to these texts, God does not simply walk away after setting creation in motion. But neither does God manipulate creation like a puppet-master. Rather, God shares creativity with the creation.

QUESTIONS

4. Does Genesis 1 describe some primeval paradise? Or does it describe our world as we find it?

5. On what do you think the author based his account of creation?

Do any of these serve as sources for us as well?

6. What order do you find in creation?

What disorder?

7. Do you agree that God shares creativity with the creation? What evidence do you find for or against that view in Genesis 1?

In life as you perceive and experience it?

Study #4

HUMAN POTENTIAL AND HUMAN LIMITATION

A DELICATE BALANCE

"What are human beings that you are mindful of them?" asks the Psalmist (8:4), implying both our insignificance in the face of the night sky (8:3), and our sense of having been given a special place in the ecology of this planet (8:5-8). Our tradition thus has the task of balancing human insignificance with human worth, and we hear our tradition blamed for erring in both directions: for making people think they are unimportant, and for making people think they are too important. When it comes to ecology, the same Christianity that for centuries was blamed for hindering the wheels of progress and science has recently been blamed for encouraging similar forces in their exploitation of nature.

Many of these criticisms have some merit. But rather than sort out truth from untruth from partial truth concerning them, I propose that we take a fresh look at human potential and human limitation in both the biblical creation stories and the literature known in Israel and its neighbors as "wisdom literature."

A PLACE FOR HUMANITY

The place of humanity in Genesis 1 seems abundantly clear: We are given dominion over all of creation (v. 26). The richly ambiguous phrase "created in the image of God" was probably originally understood as the basis for this dominion: Just as kings "erect an image of themselves in the provinces of their empire where they do not personally appear, so man is placed on earth in God's image. . . . The decisive thing about man's similarity to God, therefore, is his function in the non-human world."[5]

The permissive commands in 1:28—"be fruitful . . . fill the earth . . . subdue [lit. "trample down] . . . have dominion"—were doubtless good news to humanity in the agricultural age. If the language seems harsh, I suspect our author is guilty of nothing more than a guileless candor about the violence implicit in the relation of an agriculturally based

25

society to the earth and its creatures.* We understandably miss the
tenderness toward nature that is found in other biblical passages, and
we may prefer the language of cooperation and harmony to the language of dominion and subjugation. But which is more appropriate for
an ox yoked to a plow?

Yet as civilization has progressed, this dominion has come to have an
increasingly bitter taste in our mouths. Picking up the metaphor of
"trampling down" in Genesis 1:28, the Catholic priest and poet Gerard
Manley Hopkins wrote in 1877,

> Generations have trod, have trod, have trod;
>   And all is seared with trade; bleared, smeared with toil;
>   And wears man's smudge and shares man's smell; the soil
> Is bare now, nor can foot feel, being shod.[6]

In the century since Hopkins wrote, human devastation of the environment has accelerated; in many ways we would now be nostalgic for the
very conditions Hopkins bewailed.

We can justify the language of "dominion" in Genesis 1 not only by
an awareness of its roots in legitimizing agricultural civilization, but as
a present statement of our power and responsibility. But what direction—more specifically, what restraint—does it give us as we seek to
exercise this dominion?

Perhaps we can learn something in this matter from the second
account of creation, which begins in Genesis 2:4. This account gives
us a very different image of ourselves and our relation to the earth.
Rather than the regal image of Genesis 1 and the summons to
"subdue" the earth, the second account reminds us that we are dust,
and to dust we shall return (3:19). We are shown ourselves being
molded out of the ground like a clay mannequin, and the text draws
attention to the similarity of the Hebrew words for human being
(adam) and the ground (adamah)† from which the human creature is
formed.

---

*A violence from which some nomadic societies have recoiled. One nomadic Indian
protested the federal government's attempts at setting his tribe to agricultural pursuits
by saying, "You ask me to plow the ground. Shall I take a knife and tear my mother's
bosom?" (cited in M. Eliade, The Sacred and the Profane [New York: Harper Torchbooks,
1961], 138).
†A feminine noun; earth here is almost personified as "mother earth." (See Genesis 4:11,
where earth opens its mouth to receive the blood of Abel.)

If humanity seems more down-to-earth in this second account, then so does God. God not only forms the first human pair with his hands* (2:7, 21-22), but comes to them "walking in the garden at the time of the evening breeze" (3:8). In contrast to Genesis 1, where all of creation unfolds according to a neat, predetermined plan, the God of Genesis 2 and 3 makes decisions as he proceeds, and his responses to others' acts—and even to his own acts—appear unpremeditated. God creates a man to till the ground, then realizes Adam is lonely, then realizes the animals won't quite meet Adam's need, and so on. And what if the human couple had eaten from the tree of life before God arrived and drove them from Eden . . . ?

Moreover, unlike Genesis 1 (where God freely shares godlike attributes with humans), in Genesis 2 and 3 God appears far more jealous of his divine prerogatives. The only "godlike" attribute the first couple acquire is not what they are given, but what they contrive to steal. In relation to this, we need to ask whose "pleasure garden" Eden is, Adam's or God's? Recall that what prompts the creation of humankind in the first place is that "there was no one to till the ground" (2:5).

In giving us a God who plants, molds, and sews with his hands, and who takes walks in his private park, Genesis 2 and 3 presents us with a deity more reminiscent of pre-Jewish myths than anything else in scripture. This may explain a certain discomfort we feel with the story, but also a certain fascination. The story resembles myths in other ways as well. Along with other parts of Genesis 1 through 11 (notably the flood story), the story of the garden belongs in the company of other stories (the Babylonian Atrahasis and the Greek Prometheus come most immediately to mind) in which divinity and humanity attempt to figure out their limits with regard to each other. The humans get knowledge—a mixed blessing—but not immortality, and they are also reminded that there are limits to human self-expression. God learns the distinction between tyranny and the wise use of authority. Twice God threatens humanity with extinction, and twice he relents. The end result is a more livable arrangement for both parties.

---

*There are times in the discussion and/or translation of biblical texts when—as here, in the anthropomorphic story of Genesis 2—the use of personal pronouns to refer to God is quite natural. Indeed, the attempt to avoid pronouns altogether, or to use a mixture of male and female pronouns, can create a kind of awkwardness that obscures the story itself. In this case I have chosen to follow the example of the *New Revised Standard Version* and to use the male personal pronoun to refer to God. Of course this does not imply that God is in any sense intrinsically male.

The story of the garden, fascinating in its antiquity and in its mythic overtones, is one of surprising currency as well. For the current environmental crisis again shows us testing our limits as creatures—testing, in fact, the limits of the mandate to "have dominion" uttered in Genesis 1. There it is assumed that the mandate can coexist with the ordered, organic creation which God so carefully arranges and endows with life and creativity. But suppose we multiply and dominate to the point where we, like the overaggressive land barons rebuked by Isaiah, "are left to live alone in the midst of the land" (5:8). Suppose we pursue the permissive commands full throttle but ignore the restrictive ones. At what point in our "trampling" of the earth do we stop and see it as our mother, whose substance is one with ours? Will the creativity that God has given to humanity endanger the creativity imparted to nature? This story is still being told in our generation.

QUESTIONS

1. What aspects of Genesis 1 serve as restraints against human abuse of the earth?

2. What does the mandate to have dominion over the earth mean to you?

3. Genesis 1 glories in our godlike control; Genesis 2 is suspicious of any attempt to be like God. Which posture is more important to cultivate for us as Christians at this point in history?

WISDOM: SKILL AT LIVING

The creation stories have introduced us to the concepts of dominion and limit in fairly stark and absolute form. To give these concepts further nuances and greater utility, we will turn to the wisdom tradition in the Bible, represented by Job, Ecclesiastes, and (especially) Proverbs. It is particularly appropriate to introduce these books into a discussion of creation, since they are the ones that contemplate most directly the world as they find it.

Wisdom in the Hebrew scriptures generally refers to "skill at living."* Proverbs frequently talks about "life" as the single most important benefit gained from the acquisition of wisdom. Whoever finds wisdom, we are told, finds life (8:35); wisdom is described as a "tree of life" (3:18) and a "fountain of life" (16:22). Life here does not mean life after death, nor does it mean mere longevity or survival. Rather, it refers to all the assets—emotional, physical, mental, social, spiritual—which permit joy and security and wholeness.

Since life is the concern and promise of wisdom, it will come as no surprise if the wisdom the sages commend is found not to be purely theoretical, but to have a great deal to do with experience. Many proverbs are simply observations.

---

*The Hebrew word which is most often translated "wisdom" is *hochmah*. The word originally meant "skill," the particular expertise and experience of a metalworker, or a political adviser. It is used in Exodus 35:32-33 to describe Bezalel, whose "wisdom" consists in his ability "to devise artistic designs, to work in gold, silver, and bronze, in cutting stones for setting, and in carving wood." But for the sages of the ancient Near East, wisdom was not merely a specialized skill, important as it can be to have one, but "skill at living."

> The poor use entreaties,
>   but the rich answer roughly (18:23).
> Those whose bellies are full loathe honey,
>   but to those who are hungry everything bitter is sweet
>   (27:7, auth. trans.).

In neither case are the sages saying that this is the way the world should be, but simply that this is the way it is, and you need to be prepared for it. As Gerhard von Rad points out, "Such proverbs have the dignity and value of knowledge painfully garnered," a knowledge capable of discerning a "hidden order" behind events which seem "initially hard and perplexing . . . if they are experienced by a solitary individual without any other reference."[7]

Even when Proverbs become more prescriptive, they are not hard-and-fast rules. To treat Proverbs as hard-and-fast systematic rules is, in fact, the mark of a fool. By taking the Proverbs back to the experience from which they were derived, we gain a knowledge of the peculiar insight that produced them. And it's the insight that matters; anyone can quote a proverb but, as one of the proverbs shrewdly remarks, in the mouth of a fool it hangs limp and useless, like a lame leg (26:7).

THE WISE AND NATURE

We'll begin with Proverbs at their most pragmatic.

> Those who till their land will have plenty of food,
>   but those who follow worthless pursuits have no sense (12:11).

The land assiduously worked will provide abundant sustenance.* Here the "dominion" Genesis 1 spoke of is advocated with a frank appeal to human self-interest. This "dominion" is advocated over against an alternative course of action, also attractive to some: following "worthless pursuits," which do not cultivate a fruitful, sustaining relationship with the land.

Of particular importance to the Proverbs are domestic animals, whose participation in agriculture was essential to making it pay.

---

* It is important to remember what was said in the previous paragraph about the Proverbs not being systematic, hard-and-fast rules, lest its truths about the value of hard work be twisted into an attempt to ascribe all poverty to laziness. Proverbs itself contains a number of correctives to this view, for example: "The field of the poor may yield much food, but it is swept away through injustice" (13:23).

> No oxen, empty manger;
> strong bull, much cash (14:4, NJB).

Yet the relationship between domestic animals and their owners was moral as well as prudent.

> The righteous know the needs of their animals,
> but the mercy of the wicked is cruel (12:10).

It is the mark of being righteous that one not only has good relations with God and neighbor, but with animals; the expression "know the needs [lit., 'soul, being']" indicates empathy as well as care. We were told in Genesis 1 to "have dominion"; here we begin to get an idea of what constitutes *righteous* dominion.

The empathy expressed in Proverbs 12:10 is expanded and mingled with a lyric celebration of life on the land in a passage that a student once called the Bible's "Pastoral Symphony."

> Know well the condition of your flocks,
> and give attention to your herds;
> for riches do not last forever,
> nor a crown for all generations.
> When the grass is grown, and new growth appears,
> and the herbage of the mountains is gathered,
> the lambs will provide your clothing,
> and the goats the price of a field;
> there will be enough goats' milk for your food,
> for the food of your household
> and nourishment for your servant girls (27:23-27).

Christian theologian and farmer Richard Austin comments astutely on this passage: "Valuable in themselves, animals created relationships and responsibilities more significant than wealth, and also more enduring. Flocks and herds would respond in kind to those who cared well for them—unlike goods, which lacked vital sensibilities."[8]

Beyond the esteem with which the sages held agriculture and domestic animals, they approached nature with attitudes basic to human learning from its childhood beginnings: curiosity and play. Wisdom herself (personified as a female figure) is said to be "at play in God's presence, at play everywhere in the world, delighting to be with the children of humankind" (Prov. 8:30-31, auth. trans.). This element of play can help explain the following proverb, which sounds like a cosmic game of hide-and-seek:

> To conceal a matter is the glory of God;
>   to search it out thoroughly is the glory of kings
>   (25:2, auth. trans.).

This attitude is diametrically opposed to the fear of human discovery manifested in some religious circles.* The observation that God leaves many things "concealed" is not invoked to prohibit investigation of them, but rather to increase human glory when these same hidden things are discovered.

So far Proverbs has shown us humanity as a race which has been given dominion over nature both to fruitfully tend and to explore it. Proverbs can wax eloquent about these possibilities, and it is tempting to believe they are limitless. But Proverbs has nothing but harsh words for those who believe in the sufficiency of their own resources, mental or otherwise; in fact, it refers to such people as "fools." Proverbs lists many characteristics of the fool, but perhaps the quintessential characteristic is that fools will not accept any form of correction, pursuing instead what is "right in their own eyes" (12:15, auth. trans.).

Correction can come through the human community in a variety of ways. But it can also come through a sense of existence that recognizes the limits that exist on human understanding, authority, and competence. Proverbs doesn't let its practical, managerial skill blind it to a sense of mystery in life, a sense which is cultivated in the enigmatic numerical proverbs found toward the end of the book:

> Three things are too wonderful for me;
>   four I do not understand:
> the way of an eagle in the sky,
>   the way of a snake on a rock,
> the way of a ship on the high seas,
>   and the way of a man with a girl (30:18-19).

Note here that Proverbs holds together the natural and the human in an unbroken gaze of wonder. But life itself was a special source of wonder for the sages: "Just as you do not know how the breath comes to the bones in the mother's womb, so you do not know the work of God, who makes everything" (Eccl. 11:5). Moreover, for all its desire to train people for success, Proverbs encourages us to count on the incal-

---

*One thinks, for example, of the nineteenth-century Anglican bishop who responded to the discovery of fossils by stating that God hid them to fool the unbelievers.

culable: "The human mind plans the way, but the Lord directs the steps" (Prov. 19:21).

The insights of mystery give rise to what is perhaps Proverbs' fundamental stipulation: "The fear of the Lord is the beginning of wisdom" (9:10). I take this to be fundamentally similar to the admonition at Delphi to "know thyself": that is, know you are mortal and not divine. Wisdom begins with realizing our limitations as creatures. Proverbs therefore decisively rejects the appeal that forms the basis of many an advertising campaign, aptly summarized by a brokerage firm's recent pitch, "We believe your world should know no boundaries." As far as I can tell, they stopped that ad shortly after Black Monday—the near-crash of the Wall Street stock market in October 1988. Black Monday reminded many of us of the precariousness of an economy we take for granted, that there are—and should be—very real boundaries for our desires and egos.

QUESTIONS

4. How does Proverbs influence our understanding of what it means to "have dominion"?

5. How are human control and comprehension seen as being limited in the wisdom tradition?

Study #5

THE SABBATH WAS MADE FOR THE WORLD

THE GRACE OF DOING NOTHING

The previous decade gave us a movie which showed the Protestant tradition of the Sabbath at its most principled and strict. In *Chariots of Fire*, sprinter Eric Liddell comes from a background in which the Sabbath is devoted to God to the exclusion of both work and play. As Liddell himself tells his younger brother, "The Sabbath's not a day for playing football."

Yet, contrary to the expectations of modern viewers, the film's portrayal of Liddell ascribes to him none of the joylessness that has made "puritanical" an uncomplimentary term. In fact, Liddell both delights in his body and relates that delight to his Creator. "God made me fast," he tells his sister, "and when I run, I feel his pleasure." Liddell makes the British Olympic team, but finds that his first heat is scheduled on Sunday. His decision not to run is presented to us not as a repudiation of his running, but as an affirmation of his God. While his teammates are shown expending their energies on the track (in a manner that looks far more like work than play), Liddell is shown in church preaching on the text, "They that wait upon the Lord shall renew their strength" (Isa. 40:31, KJV).

The tradition represented by Liddell was, I believe, wrong in banishing play from the Sabbath; it is nowhere prohibited in the Bible, and would seem to provide both children and adults with rest and recreation. But Liddell's tradition was right in much else. In both spirit and action, the biblical teaching on the sabbath is one we badly need to recover for ourselves and our time.

THE SABBATH IN CREATION AND REDEMPTION

While sabbath laws occur in a number of places in the Bible, the sabbath command is best known as the fourth in the series known as the Ten Commandments. The Ten Commandments are given twice; once proclaimed directly by God at Mount Sinai (Exod. 20:1-17), and once as reviewed by Moses at the border of the land of Canaan in the book-length speech we know as Deuteronomy (5:6-21). The sabbath, of course, appears in both versions. This fact itself ought to give us pause

35

before we dismiss the sabbath as an outmoded ritual, for all of the other ten commandments have profound moral and spiritual implications.

But while both versions of the ten commandments include the sabbath command, each gives a different reason why Israel should observe it. Exodus 20:11 relates the sabbath to creation: "In six days the Lord made heaven and earth, the sea, and all that is in them, but rested the seventh day; therefore the Lord blessed the sabbath day and consecrated it." Deuteronomy 5:15, on the other hand, exhorts Israel to "remember that you were a slave in the land of Egypt, and the Lord your God brought you out from there with a mighty hand and an outstretched arm; therefore the Lord your God commanded you to keep the sabbath day."

Scholars often point out—correctly—that these divergent explanations probably point to different sources which were ultimately brought together in the final editing of Israel's laws. But what often goes unnoticed is the increased importance this double rationale gives the sabbath law. For it incorporates the sabbath into the two main perspectives from which we view God's activity: creation and redemption. The connection of the sabbath with redemption is probably less familiar and, at first, less understandable; therefore, we shall discuss it first.

SABBATH REDEMPTION AND JUSTICE

The essence of the sabbath command is simple: "You shall not do any work" (Exod. 20:10; Deut. 5:14); "you shall rest" (Exod. 34:21). It is, to be sure, a consecrated time of rest (Exod. 20:11), and we have come to associate the sabbath with church attendance and responsibilities; in some traditions, the more the better. But here and in the other sabbath commands, the Bible continually refuses to drop the other shoe and offer a religious program for the sabbath. The point is simply the cessation of work.

We will not understand the intrinsic connection between the sabbath and God's redemptive justice until we realize that the command "you shall do no work" does not address isolated individuals, but persons who have other people who do much of their work for them: sons and daughters, male and female slaves, and resident aliens. Both Exodus and Deuteronomy extend the sabbath command to include all workers, but Deuteronomy makes it clear that the rest is at least as much for them as for the boss, adding the phrase "that your male and female slave may rest as well as you" (5:14).

The fundamental human need and right not to be worked to death is therefore at the heart of the sabbath command. It should now be clear why Deuteronomy adds to its sabbath command the exhortation, "Remember that you were a slave in the land of Egypt, and the Lord your God brought you out from there with a mighty hand and an outstretched arm; therefore the Lord your God commanded you to keep the sabbath day" (5:15). Work is fundamental to life, but when it consumes all our energies it becomes oppressive. If freedom is to be truly free, it must mean freedom from the tyranny of work, and not only for ourselves, but for the entire community.*

The sabbath law is not anti-work: The six days of labor are commanded just as much as the seventh day of rest. But this day of rest helps to keep the six of work in perspective. The prophet Amos caustically described the social consequences of the loss of this perspective by putting into the mouths of Israel's merchants a speech they would never make, but which revealed their unspoken thoughts:

> "When will the new moon be over
>   so that we may sell grain;
> and the sabbath,
>   so that we may offer wheat for sale?
> We will make the ephah small and the shekel great,
>   and practice deceit with false balances,
> buying the poor for silver
>   and the needy for a pair of sandals,
>   and selling the sweepings of the wheat" (8:5-6).

In this passage, the merchants' blind pursuit of the almighty shekel ends with them cheating with false measures and balances, trafficking in human lives,† and selling the chaff and trash left after winnowing as grain. But it begins with the resentment of rest and cessation, and the desire to create a "sabbathless society," a "smoothly functioning machine . . . for coveting without limit."[9]

---

*The irony that the "new redemptive order" includes slaves will not be lost on any sensitive reader. But even they are not excluded—in fact, they are expressly included—in the divinely ordained rest. Moreover, there were attempts in Israelite law to get rid of debt—the primary cause of slavery—by an application of this same sabbath principle: "Every seventh year you shall grant a remission of debts" (Deut. 15:1).

†Apparently in Amos' time, freeborn Israelites were being sold into slavery for failure to pay even trifling debts; see also Amos 2:6, which virtually repeats the words of this passage on slavery. Although the procedure was legal, Amos rebukes it as cruel and a violation of the spirit of the covenant.

THE BELEAGUERED READER

Arguably, the phrase "sabbathless society" describes modern society to a "T." Our merchants do not have to wait for the new moon or for the sabbath; many even boast of being open twenty-four hours a day as well as seven days a week. We often speak of our members as being caught in cycles: the poor in their poverty, the middle class in the "rat race." Our technology does not bring us rest, but simply is fed into our "smoothly functioning machine" to make it run faster.

Most of us would agree with Gandhi that "there is more to life than increasing its speed."[10] Yet our very agreement will have a futile resigned quality to it, since at the same time we have to work and survive in a work environment that is often breathless and nonstop. To the beleaguered reader, the call to sabbath observance may not sound like a provision of relief, but rather an impossible extra ball to juggle.

The Israelites themselves did not always find sabbath observance easy. The reminder in one of the laws to keep the sabbath "even in plowing time and in harvest time," and the varied attempts in the biblical laws to secure debt remission and keep ancestral land in its original family (both of which were related to the sabbath) remind us that the sabbath was an ideal Israel sought to realize but never fully achieved.

Any program for sabbath observance in our age will have to be somewhat flexible. "Rest" needs to be defined over against what we customarily do as "work." In a society where most of the work was physical work, physical rest was paramount. Many of us have demanding schedules six days a week, and the sabbath should be a time when the loosening of those demands is achieved. But since many of our jobs are sedentary, might it not be that working, say, in the garden, serves a sabbatical function?

The church should call its people to a sabbath observance that is a discipline which may inconvenience our work but which is not fundamentally a burden. Above all, the primary goal of "rest" should be kept continually before our eyes; we must resist the temptation to substitute for rest a religious program every bit as compulsive as a workaholic's approach to work. Sunday school teaching is a good work, but sleeping late one morning is a lot closer to the kind of "observance" these texts have in mind.

The next section will perhaps assist us in developing a spirituality of rest. But we must not spiritualize rest too much. When my wife made a directed retreat, she was surprised to find how much emphasis the director placed on getting a lot of sleep, and on not doing too much praying (as she put it, allowing time for answers). As Psalm 127:2 reminds us, sleep itself is a precious gift from the Lord. Over the long haul, the sabbath should help us affirm that "those who wait for the Lord shall renew their strength" (Isa. 40:31).

QUESTIONS

1. Should we retain or attempt to reintroduce "blue laws"—laws regulating work and amusements on Sunday—in our community? On what basis would we do so?

2. In what way is the desire to create a "sabbathless society," a "smoothly functioning machine . . . for coveting without limit" harmful to the environment?

3. What stance should the church take toward its members and toward society as a whole in the matter of the sabbath?

A SABBATH FOR NATURE

It is not only humanity that is included in the biblical sabbath. Farm animals worked hard also, and they too were entitled to a rest. Both versions of the decalogue include "livestock," and Deuteronomy 5:14 further specifies "your ox or your donkey." In Exodus 23:12, the rationale given for the sabbath command is provision of rest for those who had done the most exacting physical labor, and domestic animals are singled out in this regard: "Six days you shall do your work, but on the seventh you shall rest, *so that your ox and your donkey may have relief, and your homeborn slave and the resident alien may be refreshed*" (author's emphasis). We are used to thinking of the sabbath as a matter of personal piety; texts such as this remind us that it is even more a matter of justice. And this justice includes the animals under our care.

The animals that worked the land needed a rest from working, and the land itself needed a rest from being worked. Immediately before the sabbath command in Exodus 23:12, Israel is told to sow and harvest the land for six years, "but the seventh year you shall let it rest and lie fallow" (23:11). The word *sabbath* is not used here, but the pattern of six of work followed by one of rest is suggestive, as is its juxtaposition with the sabbath command in the following verse. Leviticus 25:1-7 specifically refers to the land enjoying a sabbath every seventh year. Fields could not be sown or reaped, and vineyards could not be pruned or picked; what grew naturally was available for the taking by all Israelites regardless of status.

The reason for such legislation is understandable: The soil needed to replenish itself. As Baruch Levine comments,

> The practice of allowing arable land to lie fallow periodically was a necessary aspect of ancient agriculture, especially where extensive

irrigation was utilized. It served to reduce the quantity of alkalines, sodium and calcium, deposited in the soil by irrigation waters. In modern times, with the use of fertilizers, the soil is replenished through crop rotation. So, although the scheduled release of land every seventh year may smack of artificiality, expressing the cyclic thinking of the ancient Israelites, the agricultural advantages were real.[11]

It is harder to understand how this legislation was put into practice. It must have involved tremendous sacrifice on the part of Israel, comparable to a year of famine. Indeed, this law pointedly raises questions which apply to all biblical laws: At what time in Israel's history was this law created? How and to what extent was it actually enforced? These are questions that continue to be debated by scholars, the only consensus being that the laws of the Bible were developed over a long period of time. The fact that the fallow sabbath year occurs in Exodus 23 as well as Leviticus 25 (two passages generally assigned to very different stages in the development of biblical law) suggests that there were, at a minimum, serious attempts to establish this practice at several points in Israel's history.

For us, the important point is the law's recognition of the land's need to replenish itself. While these laws were certainly framed with an eye to the agricultural benefits that Levine described, the language in which they are couched speaks of the land itself as an entity with obligations and rights, which both "observes" (Lev. 25:2) and "enjoys" (Lev. 26:34, 43) its sabbaths. Perhaps the two are interrelated, and no more so than at present: We will not continue to enjoy the benefits from the land until we learn to respect it in its own right.

QUESTIONS

4. What resources today need rest in order to replenish themselves?

How can we give them rest?

5. For most of us, machines have replaced domestic animals. Would there be any benefits to the environment or to our sense of existence if everyone refrained from driving a car one day a week? *

6. The text talks about the land "observing" and "enjoying" its sabbaths, and many other biblical passages personify land or earth. What value is there in talking about the land in this way?

THE SABBATH OF CONTEMPLATION

The sabbath has a further tie to nature by being presented in the beginning of the Bible as God's culminating act of creation.

On the seventh day, God finished the work that he had done, and he rested on the seventh day from all the work that he had done. So God blessed the seventh day and hallowed it, because on it God rested from all the work he had done in creation (Gen. 2:2-3).

---

*In 1970, Americans had 1 car for every 2.5 people. In 1990, the ratio changed to one car for every 1.7 people. The result is that even though our cars are more efficient, we still use more fuel and have dirtier air than in 1970. (I am grateful to Dr. Stephen Miller for providing me with this statistic.)

If, in the second account of creation (which begins a few verses later), God had needed a rest after all that molding and planting, we would have understood the divine rest as simply a part of that account's portrayal of God in human terms. But this description of divine rest comes in the first account, where God has done nothing more than issue commands as effortless in performance as they are potent in consequence. The portrait of God in the first creation account in Genesis is very much like the one in Isaiah 40:12-31, which states that God, unlike mortals, "does not faint or grow weary" (v. 28). If this God is not tired, then what does it mean to say God rests?

A clue may be found in the conclusion of the description of the sixth day: "God saw everything that he had made, and indeed, it was very good" (1:31). God steps back and contemplates the parts in relation to the whole. I once heard a Jewish interpretation of the sabbath which applied the same pattern to us in personal terms. The sabbath gives us a chance to take our noses away from the grindstone of daily labor and to see, in broader terms, where we are headed and what we are making of the life we have been given.*

Ascribing this rest and contemplation to God stresses the godlike character and privilege of the sabbath. Recall that the first creation account (which culminates in the sabbath) is the one where human "dominion" was connected to our creation in God's image. Now we find that it is also godlike to rest, to step back, to contemplate.

It is also important to notice that what God contemplates is the same creation that we have been contemplating since the beginning of this study: earth, sea, sky, fruit trees, vegetation, sun, moon, stars, birds, fish, cattle, reptiles, humankind. To step back and look, see, smell; to consider this earth and its creatures; and to see ourselves as a part of this damaged but still harmonious whole . . . what better way to keep the sabbath?

Yet there may be even more. While our contemplation of God's world may bring us closer to God, it may be too limiting to say that the sabbath was made only for humanity. By creating the seventh day simply as a day of rest, God places a value on the pauses, the blank spaces, in life and in creation. Just as a rest in music may be as important as any of the notes, so in God's creation, hibernation may be

---

*One of the most useful "sabbatical" activities I have ever participated in is the *Intensive Journal Workshop* developed by Dr. Ira Progoff, which is valuable precisely because of the way it allows one to step back from one's life and behold it as a work on which one is engaged.

as important as procreation, deserts as important as verdant valleys, and silence as important as sounds. It is the seventh day that allows us to see creation not as ceaselessly "productive" activity, but as a matter of cycles and rhythms.

QUESTION

7. In light of this entire chapter, how would you go about creating a sabbath for yourself and your dependents? What kinds of things would you refrain from doing?

What kinds of things would you do?

Study #6

In Wisdom You Have Made Them All

A SUMMONS TO PRAISE

In the last chapter, we saw that one of the functions of the sabbath was to allow us, like God in Genesis 1, to step back and contemplate this world in its glory, detail, and interrelation. While there are a number of biblical texts that can assist us in this contemplation, I want to focus our attention on one biblical text, Psalm 104. No other single chapter of the Bible can approach it for both the quantity and the quality of what it has to say on the subject of nature. For these reasons, Psalm 104 could well be regarded as an ecological manifesto for Jews and Christians.

Calling the psalm a "manifesto"—a call to action—would suit our contemporary sense of urgency and the need for social change. But the psalm is instead a call to praise. Praise is not a substitute for action. But it is no mere prelude to activism either. Praise is an unceasing music in which all things, seen and unseen, join. We may forget to praise much, if not all, of our days, but praise has not thereby stopped. And when we do praise we merely add our voices to "the mighty chorus which the morning stars began."

> Bless the Lord, O my soul.
>   O Lord my God, you are very great.
> You are clothed with honor and majesty,
>   wrapped in light as with a garment.
> You stretch out the heavens like a tent,
>   you set the beams of your chambers on the waters,
> you make the clouds your chariot,
>   you ride on the wings of the wind,
> you make the wind your messengers,
>   fire and flame your ministers (vv. 1-4).

QUESTIONS

1. The Psalmist begins by summoning himself to praise God. What reason or reasons does he give for praising God?

2. How would you describe the relation between God and nature portrayed in these four verses?

In the next verses, the psalmist describes the primeval cataclysms from which the world emerged. That his knowledge of the earth's prehistory is symbolic rather than scientific is not remarkable. Our author shared the ancient Near-Eastern view of the earth as a kind of "oil rig" miraculously set upon the water. As we say in Study #3, these waters could represent a chaos which might threaten to engulf the world again. In Psalm 104, God not only stifles the threat posed by these waters but also transforms them into a marvelous source of life for the world.

> You set the earth on its foundations,
>   so that it shall never be shaken.
> You cover it with the deep as with a garment;
>   the waters stood above the mountains.
> At your rebuke they flee;
>   at the sound of your thunder they take to flight.

They [went up] the mountains, ran down . . . the valleys*
   to the place that you appointed for them.
You set a boundary that they may not pass,
   so that they might not again cover the earth.
You make springs gush forth in the valleys;
   they flow between the hills,
giving drink to every wild animal;
   the wild asses quench their thirst.
By the streams the birds of the air have their habitation;
   they sing among the branches.
From their lofty abode you water the mountains;
   the earth is satisfied with the fruit of your work (vv. 5-13).

QUESTIONS

3. Describe the various roles played by water in these verses.

4. Do you think these verses justify our regarding water as a special and precious gift?

---

* This parallels God's action in Genesis 1:7 of separating the waters above the sky from the waters below it. New Revised Standard Version has "they rose up *to* the mountains, ran down *to* the valleys," which would anticipate the creation of springs in verse 9.

The primeval waters are assigned to their place so that they are no longer a threat. Transformed into life-giving springs, they not only are in a "safe" place themselves, but provide habitation for others. The verses which follow not only enumerate the diversity of God's creation ("O Lord, how manifold are your works!") but attest to the divine gift of a place and a role for each that allows for, and even contributes to, the places and roles of the others ("In wisdom you have made them all").

> You cause the grass to grow for the cattle,
>   and plants for people to use,
> to bring forth food from the earth,
>   and wine to gladden the human heart,
> oil to make the face shine,
>   and bread to strengthen the human heart.
> The trees of the Lord are watered abundantly,
>   the cedars of Lebanon that he planted,
> In them the birds build their nests;
>   the stork has its home in the fir trees.
> The high mountains are for the wild goats;
>   the rocks are a refuge for the coneys. *
> You have made the moon to mark the seasons;
>   the sun knows its time for setting.
> You make darkness, and it is night,
>   when all the animals of the forest come creeping out.
> The young lions roar for their prey,
>   seeking their food from God.
> When the sun rises, they withdraw
>   and lie down in their dens.
> People go out to their work
>   and to their labor until the evening.
> O Lord, how manifold are your works!
>   In wisdom you have made them all;
>   the earth is full of your creatures.
> Yonder is the sea, great and wide,
>   creeping things innumerable are there,
>   living things both small and great.
> There go the ships,
>   and Leviathan that you formed to [play with] (vv. 14-26).

---

* Most likely, the Syrian conies [sic] (and not rabbits as might be suggested by the connotation of the English 'conies'). . . . In spite of their small size, they are related to elephants" (A. A. Anderson, *Psalms*, New Century Bible [Grand Rapids: Eerdmans, 1981], 722).

Leviathan is a sea monster, and as such can be used to represent that chaos which is overcome by the Lord in order to create a world (see the earlier verses in this psalm, also Ps. 74:14). In this psalm, it would appear that the Lord has tamed him, and that he is now the plaything of a deity. This would attest to the Creator's power (cf. Job 41:5), and is also an attempt to explain the presence of what is otherwise inexplicable in creation. New Revised Standard Version has "that you formed to sport in it," but even on this reading it is remarkable the extent to which this erstwhile representative of chaos has been domesticated. Partly because of its mythic associations with chaos and partly because Israel was not a seafaring nation, the sea as a whole appears here as something of an afterthought, "yonder."

Dr. Stephen Miller, a biologist with whom I studied this psalm, makes the following comment on this section:

It seems to me that the verse that talks of the sea as having "creeping things innumerable" is a testimony to biodiversity. The author obviously knew there were more animals there than had been seen and named by humans. These animals were obviously important to the Creator, and what better reason to praise their existence? We should have a similar attitude toward the diversity of tropical rain forests, coral reefs, etc. We have even more reason for praise (and concern) because we are beginning to appreciate how dependent we are on these ecosystems and the resources (anticancer drugs, new food sources, etc.) they represent. Estimates are that only $\frac{1}{5}$ to $\frac{1}{30}$ of the species present in tropical rain forests have been described.[12]

QUESTIONS

5. In what ways does the Psalmist assert that even places that humanity does not use are important in God's creation?

6. Since this psalm was written, in what ways has humankind extended its influence into the areas the psalm portrays as being outside our sphere of activity?

7. What does this section of the psalm say about our relations with other creatures?

The Psalmist's little appendix on the sea had interrupted the exclamation that sums up his review of the realms of nature: "O Lord, how manifold are your works! In wisdom you have made them all" (v. 24). In the following verses, the psalmist continues to portray the relation between God and the world.

These all look to you
   to give them their food in due season;
when you give to them, they gather it up;
   when you open your hand, they are filled with good
      things.
When you hide your face, they are dismayed;
   when you take away their breath, they die
   and return to their dust.
When you send forth your spirit, they are created;
   and you renew the face of the ground (vv. 27-30).

QUESTIONS

8. How would you describe the relation between God and nature portrayed in these verses?

9. In what sense is "creation" a continual activity?

The psalm concludes with language familiar from other hymns in Israel.

> May the glory of the Lord endure forever;
>   may the Lord rejoice in his works—
> who looks on the earth and it trembles,
>   who touches the mountains and they smoke.
> I will sing to the Lord as long as I live;
>   I will sing praise to my God while I have being.
> May my meditation be pleasing to him,
>   for I rejoice in the Lord.
> Let sinners be consumed from the earth,
>   and let the wicked be no more.
> Bless the Lord, O my soul (vv. 31-35).

QUESTIONS

10. How is the imagery for God different from what we have seen previously in this psalm?

    How is it similar?

11. What would appear to be the chief threat to God's rule?

For Further Reading and Action

Through these studies, we have had six sabbaths, chances to contemplate ourselves in relation to nature, and the relation of both to God, through the medium of the scriptures and the community of faith. There remains a day of work. The following are just a few steps that could be taken by persons, groups, and congregations to help preserve "this fragile earth, our island home."[13]

● Congregations may start an ongoing group whose primary concern is ecology and justice. Ideally, this group should be as inclusive as possible, representing a spectrum of vocations and concerns within the congregation. The developer as well as the committed activist has a stake in the future of our world, and the sooner environmental concerns stop being perceived as a "special interest," the better. Such a group could focus on specific issues to mobilize involvement on some local environmental issue or a recycling project; it could establish an information table and keep track of national environmental issues.

For further suggestions on what can be done on a congregational level, see the Presbyterian report, *Restoring Creation for Ecology and Justice* (Louisville: Presbyterian Church, 1990), 94-101. For further Christian reflection on the environmental crisis, see Wesley Granberg Michaelson, *A Worldly Spirituality: The Call to Redeem Life on Earth* (San Francisco: Harper and Row, 1984) and *Keeping and Healing the Creation* (Louisville: Presbyterian Church, 1989) by the Presbyterian Eco-Justice Task Force. The Presbyterian publications mentioned in this paragraph are available from Distribution Management Services, 100 Witherspoon Street, Louisville, KY 40202-1396.

● Changes in lifestyle are vital if we are to take good care of the earth. On an individual level, there is much that can be done to preserve the well-being and availability of water, air, energy, and other resources. You can make your own list of what can be done and what you need to do next. Three helpful principles in this area are thrift, organization, and thanksgiving. Thrift is an old-fashioned American virtue that we have abandoned in favor of consumerism; it is making a comeback in the form of recycling, reusing, and moving away from "disposable" products (for example, bringing cloth bags to the grocery store). Organization will allow us to do what needs to be done with greater economy and efficiency (for example, if we plan our errands, they can be accomplished in one trip instead of many). Last and perhaps most important is the cultivation of joy and thanksgiving for both the simple and not-so-simple gifts God has given us—it is the single best antidote to the impulse to get more and use more.

For further suggestions, consult the Earthworks Group's useful publication, *Fifty Simple Things You Can Do to Save the Earth* (Berkeley: Earthworks Press, 1989) or other similar publications. *Shalom Connections in Personal and Congregational Life* (Ellenwood, GA: Alternatives, 1986) is a workbook designed for groups to work through lifestyle issues and make a mutual covenant; to order call (404) 961-0102.

● There are bound to be environmental groups in your community. Your involvement in one will help you learn about environmental issues, benefit from the insights and concerns of others, and make you more aware of what options are available for action. As Proverbs remarks, "Whoever walks with the wise becomes wise" (13:20); we need to cultivate the acquaintance of those who can teach us to honor and protect this world as we live in it.

The environmental crisis has many aspects. A good introduction to the extent of the problem itself is Barry Commoner's *The Closing Circle: Nature, Man and Technology* (New York: Alfred A. Knopf, 1971). *The Next Step: Fifty More Things You Can Do to Save the Earth* (1991) is a sequel from the same authors and publisher to the book mentioned above; it focuses more on becoming environmentally active on a community level. Two regularly updated surveys of the world's ecology and its problems are World Resource Institute's *World Resources* (New York: Oxford) and Worldwatch Institute's *State of the World* (New York: Norton). Christopher Lasch's *The True and Only Heaven: Progress and Its Critics* sees in the idea of "progress" a failure to accept limits on our appetites and egos (see Study #4) and argues for a more Christian understanding of "hope."

● The last two studies affirmed that part of the biblical sabbath consisted of the contemplation of creation. Of the many books that could assist in such contemplation, I will mention only two. Aldo Leopold's *A Sand County Almanac* (San Francisco and New York: Sierra Club/Ballantine, 1972) is a treasury of observations of nature full of insight and poetic detail. Richard Cartwright Austin's four-volume Environmental Theology Series includes *The Beauty of the Lord: Awakening the Senses* (Atlanta: John Knox, 1988) which not only revitalizes our appreciation of natural beauty but does so by drawing on the insights of Jonathan Edwards (1703-1758), thus bringing the man who was perhaps America's greatest theologian out of ill-deserved neglect. All books in this series are now distributed by Austin's own publishing company: Creekside Press, P. O. Box 331, Abingdon, VA 24210. The other books are *Baptized into Wilderness: A Christian Perspective on John Muir* (1987), *Hope for the Land: Nature and the Bible* (1988), and *Reclaiming America: Restoring Nature to Culture* (1990).

Endnotes

1. J. R. Baxter, Jr., in *Songs We Sing*, ed. J. Filbert (Fort Worth, TX: Filbert, 1954), 243. Used by permission of Stamps-Baxter Music.

2. "Some Thoughts," in *God in the Dock: Essays in Theology and Ethics*, ed. W. Hooper (Grand Rapids, MI: Eerdmans, 1970), 150.

3. Mary Taylor, quoted in Robert Bellah, et al., *Habits of the Heart: Individualism and Commitment in American Life* (Berkeley: University of California Press, 1985), 193. "Mary Taylor" is a pseudonym, this being the standard practice with the subjects interviewed in *Habits* (p. 309).

4. Richard Austin, *Hope for the Land: Nature in the Bible* (Atlanta: John Knox, 1988), 48 (italics mine).

5. Gerhard von Rad, *Genesis*, rev. ed.; original trans. J. H. Marks (Philadelphia: Westminster, 1972), 60.

6. "God's Grandeur," in *The Poems of Gerard Manley Hopkins*, 4th ed., ed. W. H. Gardner and N. H. MacKenzie (London: Oxford University, 1970), 66.

7. *Old Testament Theology*, 2 vols., trans. D. M. G. Stalker (New York: Harper & Row, 1962), 1:420.

8. *Hope for the Land*, 93.

9. Walter Brueggemann, *The Land*, Overtures to Biblical Theology 1 (Philadelphia: Fortress, 1977), 65.

10. Attributed to Mahatma Gandhi on a poster in St. Ann's Episcopal Church, Nashville, TN. While I could not find the source of this aphorism, the sentiment is quite characteristic of Gandhi's thoughts on modern industry and technology; see the section "Blueprint for a Better Life" in *The Essential Gandhi*, ed. L. Fischer (New York: Random House, 1962), 283-302.

11. *Leviticus*, The JPS Torah Commentary (Philadelphia: Jewish Publication Society, 1989), 272.

12. Private communication.

13. "The Holy Eucharist: Rite Two," *The Book of Common Prayer: The Episcopal Church* (New York: Seabury Press, 1977), 370.